D1175548

Junior Drug Awareness
Heroin

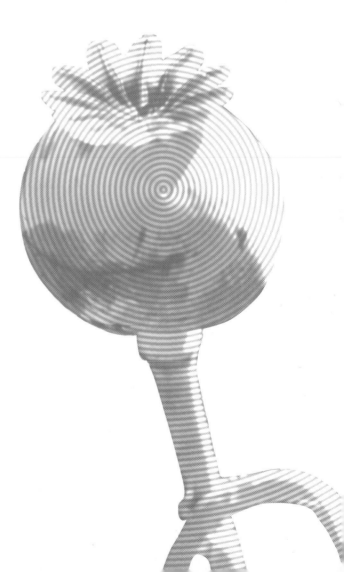

Junior Drug Awareness

Heroin

Introduction by **BARRY R. McCAFFREY**
Director, Office of National Drug Control Policy

Foreword by **STEVEN L. JAFFE, M.D.**
Professor of Child and Adolescent Psychiatry,
Emory University

Jim Gallagher

Chelsea House Publishers
Philadelphia

CHELSEA HOUSE PUBLISHERS
Editor in Chief Stephen Reginald
Production Manager Pamela Loos
Director of Photography Judy L. Hasday
Art Director Sara Davis
Managing Editor James D. Gallagher
Senior Production Editor Lisa Chippendale

Staff for HEROIN
Senior Editor Therese De Angelis
Associate Art Director/Designer Takeshi Takahashi
Picture Researcher Patricia Burns
Cover Illustration/Design Takeshi Takahashi

First Printing
1 3 5 7 9 8 6 4 2

Library of Congress Cataloging-in-Publication Data

Gallagher, Jim, 1969-
Heroin / by Jim Gallagher.
80 pp.   cm. — (Junior drug awareness)
Includes bibliographical references and index.
Summary: Examines the history, nature, sources, and
effects of heroin, the dangers of its use, and treatment
for addiction to it.
ISBN 0-7910-5181-1
1. Heroin—Juvenile literature. 2. Heroin habit—Prevention—Juvenile literature. 3. Heroin habit—Treatment—Juvenile literature. [1. Heroin. 2. Drug abuse.] I.
Title. II. Series.
HV5822.H4G35   1998
362.29'3—dc21   98-44920
                                            CIP
                                            AC

CONTENTS

by Barry R. McCaffrey
Director, Office of National
Drug Control Policy

STAYING AWAY FROM ILLEGAL DRUGS, TOBACCO PRODUCTS, AND ALCOHOL

Good health allows you to be as strong, happy, smart, and skillful as you can possibly be. The worst thing about illegal drugs is that they damage people from the inside. Our bodies and minds are wonderful, complicated systems that run like finely tuned machines when we take care of ourselves.

Doctors prescribe legal drugs, called medicines, to heal us when we become sick, but dangerous chemicals that are not recommended by doctors, nurses, or pharmacists are called illegal drugs. These drugs cannot be bought in stores because they harm different organs of the body, causing illness or even death. Illegal drugs, such as marijuana, cocaine or "crack," heroin, methamphetamine ("meth"), and other dangerous substances are against the law because they affect our ability to think, work, play, sleep, or eat.

If anyone ever offers you illegal drugs or any kind of pills, liquids, substances to smoke, or shots to inject into your body, tell them you're not interested. You should report drug pushers—people who distribute these poisons—to parents, teachers, police, coaches, clergy, or other adults whom you trust.

Cigarettes and alcohol are also illegal for youngsters. Tobacco products and drinks like wine, beer, and liquor are particularly harmful for children and teenagers because their bodies, especially their nervous systems, are still developing. For this reason, young people are more likely to be hurt by illicit drugs—including cigarettes and alcohol. These two products kill more people—from cancer and automobile accidents caused by intoxicated drivers—than all other drugs combined. We say about drug use: "Users are losers." Be a winner and stay away from illegal drugs, tobacco products, and alcoholic beverages.

Here are four reasons why you shouldn't use illegal drugs:

- Illegal drugs can cause brain damage.
- Illegal drugs are "psychoactive." This means that they change your personality or the way you feel. They also impair your judgment. While under the influence of drugs, you are more likely to endanger your life or someone else's. You will also be less able to protect yourself from danger.
- Many illegal drugs are addictive, which means that once a person starts taking them, stopping is extremely difficult. An addict's body craves the drug and becomes dependent upon it. The illegal drug–user may become sick if the drug is discontinued and so may become a slave to drugs.

- Some drugs, called "gateway" substances, can lead a person to take more dangerous drugs. For example, a 12-year-old who smokes marijuana is 79 times more likely to have an addiction problem later in life than a child who never tries marijuana.

Here are some reasons why you shouldn't drink alcoholic beverages, including beer and wine coolers:

- Alcohol is the second leading cause of death in our country. More than 100,000 people die every year because of drinking.
- Adolescents are twice as likely as adults to be involved in fatal alcohol-related car crashes.
- Half of all assaults against girls or women involve alcohol.
- Drinking is illegal if you are under the age of 21. You could be arrested for this crime.

Here are three reasons why you shouldn't smoke cigarettes:

- Nicotine is highly addictive. Once you start smoking, it is very hard to stop, and smoking cigarettes causes lung cancer and other diseases. Tobacco- and nicotine-related diseases kill more than 400,000 people every year.
- Each day, 3,000 kids begin smoking. One-third of these youngsters will probably have their lives shortened because of tobacco use.
- Children who smoke cigarettes are almost six times more likely to use other illegal drugs than kids who don't smoke.

If your parents haven't told you how they feel about the dangers of illegal drugs, ask them. One of every 10 kids aged 12 to 17 are using illegal drugs. They do not understand the risks they are taking with their health and their lives. However, the vast majority of young people in America are smart enough to figure out that drugs, cigarettes, and alcohol could rob them of their future. Be your body's best friend: guard your mental and physical health by staying away from drugs.

WHY SHOULD I LEARN ABOUT DRUGS?

Steven L. Jaffe, M.D.
Professor of Child and Adolescent Psychiatry,
Emory University

Your grandparents and great-grandparents did not think much about "drug awareness." That's because drugs, to most of them, simply meant "medicine."

Of the three types of drugs, medicine is the good type. Medicines such as penicillin and aspirin promote healing and help sick people get better.

Another type of drug is obviously bad for you because it is poison. Then there are the kind of drugs that fool you, such as marijuana and LSD. They make you feel good, but they harm your body and brain.

Our great crisis today is that this third category of drugs has become widely abused. Drugs of abuse are everywhere, not just in rough neighborhoods. Many teens are introduced to drugs by older brothers, sisters, friends, or even friends' parents. Some people may use only a little bit of a drug, but others who inherited a tendency to become addicted may move on to using drugs all the time. If a family member is or was an alcoholic or an addict, a young person is at greater risk of becoming one.

Drug abuse can weaken us physically. Worse, it can cause permanent mental damage. Our brain is the most important part of our body. Our thoughts, hopes, wishes, feelings, and memories are located there, within 100 billion nerve cells. Alcohol and drugs that are abused will harm—and even destroy—these cells. During the teen years, your brain continues to develop and grow, but drugs and alcohol can impair this growth.

I treat all types of teenagers at my hospital programs and in my office. Many suffer from depression or anxiety. A lot of them abuse drugs and alcohol, and this makes their depression or fears worse. I have celebrated birthdays and high school graduations with many of my patients. But I have also been to sad funerals for others who have died from problems with drug abuse.

Doctors understand more about drugs today than ever before. We've learned that some substances (even some foods) that we once thought were harmless can actually cause health problems. And for some people, medicines that help relieve one symptom might cause problems in other ways. This is because each person's body chemistry and immune system are different.

For all of these reasons, drug awareness is important for everyone. We need to learn which drugs to avoid or question— not only the destructive, illegal drugs we hear so much about in the news, but also ordinary medicines we buy at the supermarket or pharmacy. We need to understand that even "good" drugs can hurt us if they are not used correctly. If we take any drug without a doctor's advice, we are taking a risk.

Drug awareness enables you to make good decisions. It allows you to become powerful and strong and have a meaningful life!

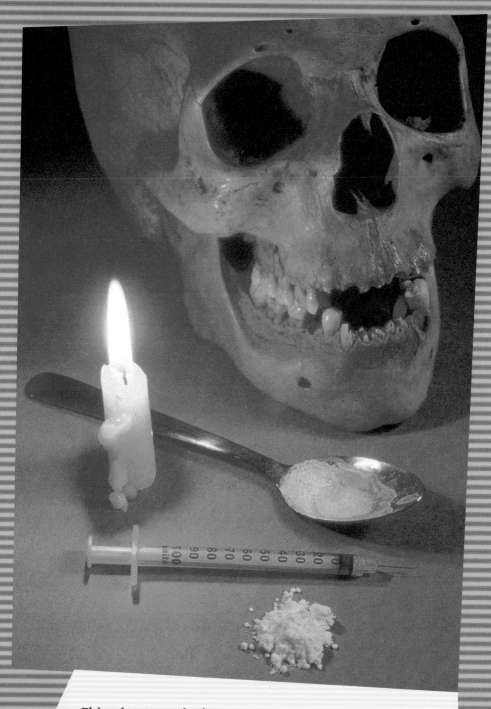

This photograph shows some of the paraphernalia (devices or equipment) employed by heroin users to inject the drug. Heroin can be deadly; users often die from overdoses or diseases spread by dirty needles.

WHO USES HEROIN?

Jonathan Melvoin was a successful musician who seemed to have everything going for him. He was happily married, and he had a young child. The popular alternative rock band Smashing Pumpkins had invited the keyboard player to perform with the group during its world tour. But the good times ended on July 12, 1996, when Melvoin, age 34, overdosed on **heroin,** a powerful narcotic drug that slowed his heart and breathing until they stopped.

Melvoin and another member of Smashing Pumpkins, drummer Jimmy Chamberlain, had been using heroin together during the tour. At the end of June, Melvoin and Chamberlain both ended up in the hospital from overdoses of heroin, but they survived. Was Melvoin thinking about that overdose when he decided to inject the drug again on July 12? Probably not, but no one will ever know. He died in his New York City hotel room that night, while Chamberlain lay passed out nearby.

Melvoin is just one of many celebrities whose lives have been cut short by heroin, one of the most **addictive** and dangerous drugs known. Actor Robert Downey Jr. and singer Courtney Love (the wife of suicide victim Kurt Cobain, lead singer of the band Nirvana and a chronic heroin user) have also had well-publicized battles with heroin addiction. Read the story in this chapter about the many other popular actors and musicians who died while they were still young because they were addicted to heroin.

But you don't have to be famous to abuse heroin. According to the U.S. Drug Enforcement Agency (DEA), the number of heroin-related incidents reported in U.S. hospital emergency rooms more than doubled between 1990 and 1995. More than 800,000 Americans are regular heroin users, according to the U.S. government. About 2.5 million people in the United States have at least tried heroin during their lifetimes—some of them before high school. Although the number of preteens who try heroin is still very low, its use has steadily increased among eighth-graders since 1994.

What Is Heroin?

Heroin is a powerful and illegal drug that is distilled from the sap of a plant called the opium poppy. The scientific name for this plant is *Papaver somniferum,* which means "sleep-inducing poppy." The name comes from the drowsy, dreamlike feeling that is one of the major effects of the drug. Heroin is one of a group of drugs called **opiates,** which depress (slow) the body's central nervous system and help relieve pain. Other opiates include opium, **morphine,** and **codeine.**

The opium poppy flourishes in dry, warm climates. Today, most of the world's supply of this plant is grown in two regions. One area, known as the "Golden Triangle," includes the Southeast Asian nations of Myanmar, Thailand, and Laos. Another major opium-producing area is known as the "Golden Crescent" and includes Iran, Afghanistan, and Pakistan. Colombia, South America, is also a major supplier of opium poppies.

About three months after poppy seeds are planted, the plant's flowers bloom. Inside each flower is an egg-shaped seed pod that contains a milky sap. This is opium in its crudest form. When the pods are cut, the sap oozes out and turns darker and thicker, forming a brownish-black gum. The gum is collected and sent to a refinery.

In a legal refinery, the raw opium is distilled into a substance called morphine, a purer form of opium that is used as a strong painkiller by doctors. Morphine can also be abused like heroin if used incorrectly or without a prescription.

In an illegal refinery, the sap of opium plants is processed much the same way, but because these refineries are producing an illegal drug, there are few controls to regulate the purity of the finished product. In addition, one processing stage for heroin involves two dangerous chemicals, ether and hydrochloric acid. These

(continued on p. 18)

Actor River Phoenix was only 23 when he died in 1993. His death was caused by an overdose of several drugs, including heroin.

Heroin and Popular Entertainers

Heroin use has been linked with entertainers and musicians since the drug was first developed at the end of the 19th century. Heroin was popularly associated with American jazz musicians and singers during the 1920s and 1930s. Billie Holiday was considered the best jazz singer of her time. Yet she struggled with heroin addiction most of her life. Holiday died from health problems that stemmed from heroin and alcohol abuse. The great saxophonist Charlie Parker developed a new style of jazz called "bebop." When Parker died at age 35 of a heart attack partly due to heavy heroin use, the coroner remarked that the jazzman had the body of a man 20 years older.

Two of the most popular rock singers of the 1960s died from heroin overdoses. Janis Joplin, whose hit songs included "Me and Bobby McGee" and "Piece of My Heart," died in her hotel room in September 1970 from a heroin overdose. Jim Morrison, the lead singer of the popular rock band the Doors, was found dead one July morning from a heroin overdose.

Keith Richards, a guitarist with the Rolling Stones, had a history of heroin abuse. During the 1970s, Richards was arrested for drug offenses 10 times. In 1979, heroin claimed the life of 21-year-old British punk rocker Sid Vicious, the lead singer of the Sex Pistols.

Comedian John Belushi, who rocketed to fame in the 1970s as a regular on *Saturday Night Live,* injected a **speedball**—a combination of heroin and cocaine—into his veins in March 1982. The powerful drug cocktail stopped his heart and killed him. He was 33 years old.

During the late 1980s and early 1990s, heroin claimed the lives of a number of musicians and entertainers. The drug killed Hillel Slovak, the 25-year-old lead guitarist of the band Red Hot Chili Peppers, in 1988. Kurt Cobain, the lead singer for Nirvana, was only 26 when he committed suicide in 1994. He had struggled for a long time with a heroin addiction. The week before his death, he nearly died of an overdose.

Blind Melon band member Shannon Hoon died of a heroin overdose in 1995. The same year, Jerry Garcia, the lead singer for the legendary band the Grateful Dead, died of complications while trying to overcome his heroin addiction. In 1997, fashion photographer David Sorrenti died from heroin abuse. Sorrenti was one of the developers of what is called the "heroin chic" look in fashion photography—extremely thin models who are pale and hollow-eyed to resemble chronic heroin users.

(continued from p. 15)

chemicals can explode and destroy the entire building where opium is being distilled, or kill those inside. When this refining process is complete, the final product is a fluffy white powder: heroin.

After being processed, heroin is distributed throughout the world, usually in the form of "bricks" weighing one kilogram (2.2 pounds). These bricks, also called "kilos," are packaged and sold illegally for enormous amounts of money—between $100,000 and $120,000, according to the DEA. A kilo of heroin is often divided by a local dealer into small bags containing an ounce or two of the drug. These bags usually cost $5 to $100. By the time the heroin reaches the street, its value has increased 10 times.

Until recently, heroin sold illegally in the United States was usually heavily diluted, or "cut," by drug dealers who wanted to make more money and have their drug supply last longer. To do this, dealers add white, powdery substances that look like the drug, such as sugar, flour, or rat poison. Most street heroin before 1990 was rarely even 10 percent pure. Beginning in the 1990s, however, heroin became more widely produced. As a result, more was available, and the purity rose sharply, to 50 or 60 percent. This very strong heroin is often smoked or inhaled ("snorted") like cocaine, rather than taken through the more common method of injection.

Who Uses Heroin?

Unfortunately, because heroin has become more

readily available and more potent, more young people than ever are trying it. The Office of National Drug Control Policy at the White House (ONDCP) noted in 1997 that heroin use is increasing or is already high in every part of the country. The number of young and new users who snort the more powerful form of the drug is increasing. And those who begin by snorting heroin often end up injecting it regularly.

As a result, many communities where heroin use was once uncommon are now experiencing firsthand the dangers of abusing the drug. For example, Plano, Texas, is considered one of the nation's safest cities; yet in 1997, 11 residents died of heroin overdoses. In Orlando, Florida, 48 people died of heroin overdoses in 1995 and 1996; 10 of these victims were 21 or younger.

Heroin is highly addictive. Once a person starts using the drug, stopping is extremely difficult for both physical and psychological reasons. In Chapters 3 and 4, we will examine the ways in which heroin affects the user's mind and body.

This painting from 1891 shows two Iranians igniting and smoking opium. Smoking the drug produces a stronger effect than eating or drinking the juice of the opium plant.

THE HISTORY OF HEROIN

Opium use is not new. For thousands of years, the juice found in the opium poppy has been used to reduce pain, induce sleep, and inspire creativity. The ancient people known as the Sumerians were the first to use opium about 5,000 years ago, around 3,400 B.C. The Sumerians called the poppy "Hul Gil," meaning "the joy plant," because of its calming, pleasurable effects. The Sumerians' knowledge of opium was passed on to later cultures that developed in the Middle East, such as the Assyrians, the Babylonians, and the Egyptians.

The Magic Drug

In ancient Egypt, the opium poppy was called *thebacium,* because it was grown in huge fields near the capital city of Thebes. Opium was very popular in Egyptian civilization. Priests and physicians praised the "magic" properties of the poppy juice, and it became a commonly used household drug.

Egyptian traders brought the poppy across the Mediterranean Sea to Greece and Rome. Hippocrates (460–377 B.C.), a Greek physician who is often called the "father of medicine," was one of the first people to write about opium's medicinal value. He described its usefulness as a painkiller and in treating internal diseases, and he prescribed it regularly. When Alexander the Great expanded the Greek empire around 330 B.C., opium was introduced to the people of Persia (present-day Iran) and India.

By the seventh century A.D., the Turkish and Islamic cultures of western Asia had discovered that igniting and smoking opium juices produced a stronger effect than eating or drinking it in a potion. The Turks and Arabs began cultivating large poppy fields, and merchants traded poppy plants with their customers in the Far East, especially China.

The Dangerous Drug

By the 11th century, Islamic doctors knew that opium was addictive, and that a user needed more and more to gain the same effects experienced previously. (This means that the body has developed a **tolerance** to the drug.) In the 14th century, Arab scientists noted that the drug "weakened" the mind of regular users. It was already commonly known that even a single use could cause death.

But opium use remained popular in Middle Eastern countries for centuries. During the Middle Ages, however, its use declined in Europe because of disapproval by the Catholic Church. The Catholic Church was very powerful and had strict rules about medicine. Church scholars mistrusted anything coming from the mysterious non-Christian countries of the Far and Middle East. Not until the mid-1500s was opium reintroduced to Europeans as a medicine. A Swiss physician named Paracelsus combined opium, citrus juice, and gold powder into a pill, which he called **laudanum.** He claimed that this drug could cure any pain-producing disease, and even heal people who were near death. Before long, laudanum and other opium combinations had become remedies, widely used throughout Europe for nearly every illness.

The lure of opium is so powerful that in the 19th century it sparked two wars, known as the Opium Wars, between China and Great Britain. Smoking opium became so prevalent in the cities along the coast of China that in 1799 the emperor banned opium trade completely. But the drug continued to flow into the country illegally. The largest importer of the 19th century was the British East India Company, a private commercial firm. By 1830, nearly 2,000 tons of opium were being imported into the country, and millions of Chinese had become addicted to opium.

In 1838, the British government pressured Chinese leaders to legalize opium so that Great Britain's profits from the opium trade would increase. Instead, the

Chinese emperor seized and destroyed imported supplies of the drug and executed opium users. Angered by China's actions, Great Britain sent warships to China's coast in 1839. In 1842, the defeated Chinese were forced to sign a treaty with the British that required them to pay a huge fine and give up some of their own seaports to Great Britain.

A second war began in 1856 when Chinese police boarded a British ship in the port of Canton and accused the crew of smuggling opium. China was defeated a second time, and the Treaty of Tianjin in 1858 forced China to legalize opium.

A New Way to Use Opium

In 1803, a German scientist named Frederick Sertuerner decided to try to find the specific chemicals in opium that made it such a powerful painkiller. He derived a crystal **alkaloid** (an organic substance containing nitrogen) that was so potent that an extremely small amount produced very strong effects. Sertuerner named this concentrated drug morphine, after an ancient Greek deity, Morpheus, the god of dreams and sleep.

Physicians of the time believed that opium had finally been perfected and tamed, and they praised morphine as "God's own medicine." When a Scottish doctor invented the hypodermic syringe during the 1840s, the device allowed physicians to administer morphine in a whole new way. They learned that the injected drug affected their patients immediately, because it was quickly absorbed into the bloodstream. Injecting morphine made the drug's effects three times more powerful than ingesting (eating) it. Because using a hypodermic syringe initially required skill and practice, injecting morphine was restricted to physicians. Before long, however, addicts began using the drug in the same way.

Meanwhile, opium-based medications for recreational use were growing increasingly popular. Literary figures such as Samuel Taylor Coleridge and Edgar Allan Poe used the drug to induce a feeling of euphoria (an extreme sense of happiness or well-being), which they thought increased their creative powers. Others, such as English writer Thomas De Quincey, criticized the widespread use of opiates. In 1822, De Quincey published an account of his own opium addiction. He called it *Confessions of an English Opium-Eater.* He explained that he had started using laudanum for medicinal purposes but found himself fighting a fierce craving for the drug. He described how his body developed a tolerance to the drug and that he experienced terrible symptoms of withdrawal when he attempted to stop using it. However, despite the interest in De Quincey's book and the growing awareness of the addictive qualities of morphine and opium, most people continued to use a variety of laudanum preparations.

In the United States, the opium problem increased after thousands of Chinese immigrants entered the country to help build railroads and work the mines in California and other western states. These immigrants brought with them the practice of smoking opium. As a result, imports of opium into the United States increased

2,000 percent between 1830 and 1870.

The Problem of Addiction

Around the same time, morphine addiction was also becoming a problem. During the American Civil War, the drug was used so often to treat wounded soldiers that the resulting increase in addictions was called "the army disease." Chemists began searching for a way to refine the drug to keep its painkilling qualities but not its addictive side effects.

Why Is It Called Heroin?

After the Bayer Company discovered that diacetylmorphine was a stronger painkiller than morphine, the new drug was pronounced a "heroine" (a female hero) in the war against pain. The name was eventually shortened to "heroin."

After the Civil War ended in 1865, government authorities on the West Coast began to worry about the effects of drug addiction on their growing communities. They began to pass laws that would prohibit opium. In 1883 and in 1890, the U.S. Congress imposed tariffs (taxes) on opium and morphine. In 1905, it banned opium use altogether. Two years later, the Pure Food and Drug Act required that all manufacturers label the contents of patent medicines—which often included opiates or alcohol. As a result, opiate-based preparations became less popular.

Around this time, one of the scientists who had continued to search for a less addictive form of opium synthesized a new drug from morphine. Heinrich Dreser, a chemist with the Bayer Company (the German drug company that developed aspirin), discovered that the new substance, **diacetylmorphine,** was more potent than morphine but less likely to produce nausea and other side effects. At first, doctors believed that it could be used in place of morphine and could end addiction to the drug.

However, the Bayer Company quickly discovered it had made a terrible mistake. Although heroin was a stronger painkiller than morphine, it was even more addictive and more dangerous. Bayer immediately

A laborer in Afghanistan uses a special knife to score (cut) opium poppy heads and extract the milky sap. It takes 10 tons of opium to produce one ton of heroin.

stopped making the drug, but it was too late. People in private laboratories had already learned how to process morphine into heroin, and use of the new drug spread throughout the world.

Taking Legal Action

In 1909, the United States banned all imports of opium into the country. The government also argued that distribution of narcotics should be restricted around the world. Representatives of other countries, including Great Britain and other European nations, agreed. In 1914, Congress passed the Harrison Narcotics Act, which curbed the distribution of cocaine and other dangerous drugs in the United States. The number of Americans who used opiates, even occasionally, dropped sharply.

But the Harrison Narcotics Act did not ban heroin outright. The drug was so new that the government still didn't officially recognize its addictive properties. As a result, opium, morphine, and cocaine addicts simply switched to a legal alternative: heroin. Others began using heroin as an alternative to alcohol when the 18th Amendment to the U.S. Constitution banned the manufacture and sale of alcoholic beverages in 1920. (The period that the 18th Amendment was in effect, from 1920 to 1933, is commonly called Prohibition.)

Finally, in 1924, the U.S. government banned heroin distribution. But the new law created another problem. It forced addicts to buy on the "black market" from street dealers and led to a criminal underworld that specialized in distributing narcotics. Still, by the mid-1930s, heroin's popularity had declined because of federal crackdowns on illegal sales and because Prohibition was no longer in effect.

World War II disrupted international opium smuggling. When the war ended in 1945, it was estimated that the number of heroin addicts in the United States had dropped to 50,000. In the years after World War II, however, the illegal flow of heroin into the United States exploded. In the late 1950s, there were approximately 100,000 heroin addicts in America—twice the number of 15 years earlier. By 1975, there were 750,000 heroin addicts in America—and the number was increasing.

An Ongoing Problem

In the late 1970s the United States launched an all-out effort to stop heroin imports. The increased government pressure on opium growers, heroin dealers, and drug addicts helped to reduce the number of heroin addicts in the United States to about 500,000 by the mid-1980s. But in recent years heroin has become widely available and less expensive. Because the heroin sold today is usually much purer than in previous years, smoking (rather than injecting) the drug has also become popular.

In 1993, the ONDCP estimated that there were about 200,000 casual users of heroin and 780,000 addicts in the United States. That number had increased to 320,000 casual users and 810,000 addicts by 1995.

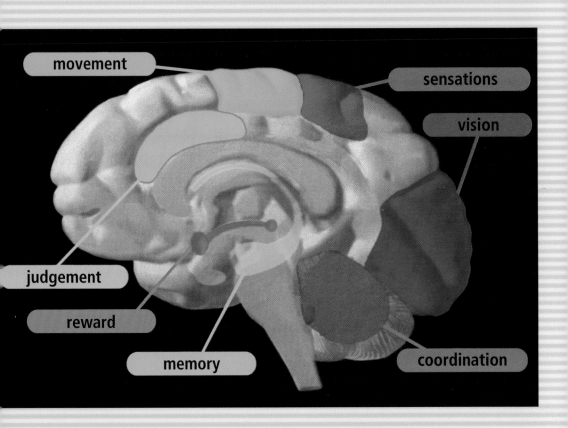

movement

sensations

vision

judgement

reward

memory

coordination

The brain is a very complicated organ. Each of its regions has a special job to do. Drugs like heroin prevent the brain from functioning the way it should. This map shows you where some of the regions are located and what their jobs are.

HOW DOES HEROIN WORK?

A lthough people have known for thousands of years about the feelings of pleasure and relaxation produced by opiates, it was only about 30 years ago that scientists discovered how opiates work. That was when chemists began trying to create an opiate that would be less addictive than morphine, codeine, and heroin.

An opiate compound made in a laboratory and not directly from the poppy plant is called an **opioid**. Researchers learned a curious fact about one of the opioids they created. Its chemical structure was similar to other opiates, but when it was injected, it did not seem to produce the same effects as the opiates. In addition, experiments showed that if the new compound was taken together with an opiate, or was given to a person who had recently taken an opiate, it would block the

effects of that drug. This compound and others like it were named **opiate antagonists.**

How Opiates Reach the Brain

The development of opiate antagonists led researchers to come up with a new theory about how heroin and other opiates affect the brain and body. They believed that an opiate travels through the bloodstream to the brain. There, it attaches itself to special areas, called **receptor sites,** on the long nerves or **neurons** that make up part of the brain and central nervous system. The analgesic (pain-relieving) and euphoric (pleasure-producing) effects of opiates seemed to be "switched on" when the connections between drug and nerve cells were made.

In 1973, researchers isolated these special nerve endings in the human brain. They called them **opiate receptors,** because they "receive" opiates into the brain. But the researchers still had questions. They didn't understand why the brain would develop special receptors for opiates, which are not produced inside the body. Could it be that the receptors were meant to receive natural substances that *do* occur in the body? Did opiates resemble these substances and thus fit the receptor sites?

"Natural Opiates"

The answer to both questions was yes, and it came two years later in 1975. That year, researchers in Aberdeen, Scotland, and at the Johns Hopkins University in Maryland identified special chemicals manufactured in the brain that linked with the opiate receptors. These tiny protein molecules are called **endorphins,** from the Greek words meaning "morphine inside."

Endorphins are a kind of **neurotransmitter,** a chemical that is released by neurons to carry messages to other nerve cells. When neurons "fire," the neurotransmitters they release travel through the bloodstream to attach themselves to other receptor sites in the body. In this way, neurotransmitters help regulate our responses to stress, pain, and other internal and external events that affect our well-being.

When you exercise hard or have a very stressful day, the body produces more endorphins, which flood the **synapses** (spaces) between neurons and inhibit them from sending pain messages to the brain. Maybe you have heard about marathon runners or other athletes experiencing a pleasurable feeling after a strenuous workout that might otherwise cause physical pain. This pleasant sensation is known as a "runner's high." The high is produced by endorphins. For this reason, endorphins are often called the "natural opiates" of the body.

How Opiates Mimic Endorphins

To figure out exactly what heroin does to the body, scientists mapped out the areas where opiate receptors are located. They discovered that the places where opiate receptors are most concentrated are those associated with the perception of pain.

Morphine and other opiates are often called painkillers, but they do not actually remove pain.

Instead, they help the body to ignore it. For example, say you accidentally touch a hot stove. The neurons in your hand instantly transmit the message through the spinal cord to the brain, which registers the pain (ouch!). If you had morphine or another opiate in your body, it would not keep you from feeling pain or getting burned. Instead, it would block the pain messages coming to the brain from your hand, so that the pain would seem less intense. This is why a person suffering great pain who is given morphine may remark that he or she can still feel the pain, almost like a dull ache, but is not bothered by it.

In addition to the pain centers of the brain, opiate receptors are also concentrated in other regions. For example, a person using opiates usually has constricted, or very small, pupils. This happens because a great number of opiate receptors are located in the part of the brain responsible for controlling the muscles in the eye. Another group of opiate receptors is found in the **limbic system**—the area that controls emotions. Opiates change the limbic system to produce increased feelings of pleasure, relaxation, and contentment.

Another concentration of opiate receptors occurs in the **brain stem,** which controls things your body does automatically, such as breathing and coughing. This explains why an overdose of opiates can slow one's breathing or even stop it completely, causing death.

What Is Addiction?

In November 1997, doctors at a seminar held by the

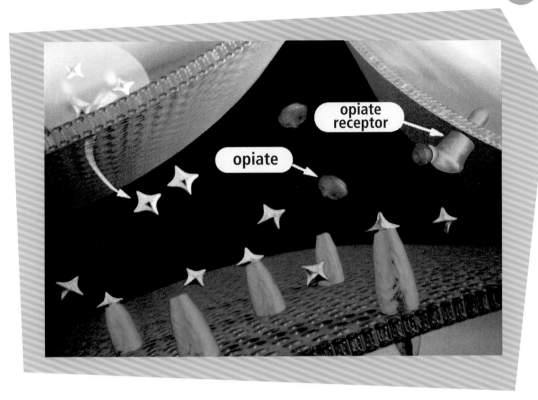

This diagram shows a close-up of a synapse (the space between nerve endings) in the brain. Opiates like heroin (purple) attach themselves to opiate receptors (green) on the ends of neurons. The orange molecules represent dopamine, a neurotransmitter, which attaches to its own receptors (blue) on another neuron.

National Institutes of Health argued that heroin addiction should be treated as a disease. Lewis Judd, the chairman of the Department of Psychiatry at the University of California at San Diego, said, "Opiate addiction is a mental disorder and basically is a brain-related disease." He made clear that being addicted to opiates does not mean that a person is weak or immoral.

Why would doctors say that drug addiction is a disease? We usually think of a disease as a sickness that

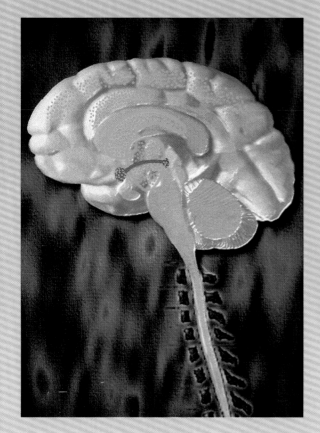

These drawings show the regions of the brain that are affected by opiates. The green dots in the picture on the left show where opiate receptors are located in the brain and spinal cord. The drawing on the right shows the regions of the brain that are responsible for addiction to and dependence on heroin and

impairs a living organism's normal function. Diseases can usually be recognized by specific symptoms. Although this sounds like what we've learned about heroin addiction so far, most diseases are the result of a viral infection or defective genetic material. People don't choose to get tuberculosis or muscular dystrophy, for example, but they do choose to take drugs.

This is true. But it is important to remember that even though a heroin user may choose to take the drug, he or she does not choose to become **physically and**

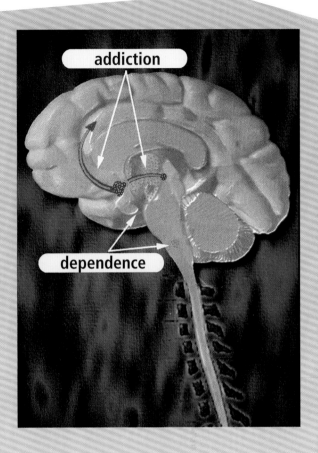

addiction

dependence

other opiates. The red areas represent a region known as the "reward pathway," or pleasure center. Opiates act on this region of the brain as well. Once someone becomes dependent on an opiate, the green areas need the drug to function normally. If they do not get it, withdrawal occurs.

psychologically dependent on it. Addiction happens involuntarily. This is why mental health professionals explain that *using* an addictive drug is not a disease, but *addiction* to the drug is a disease. Heroin addiction develops automatically after people who are **predisposed** to addiction begin using the drug.

Heroin is one of the toughest addictions to overcome, for two reasons. One, it creates a powerful psychological craving; that is, the user craves the feeling of well-being that the drug produces. Two, long-term hero-

in use actually changes the way nerve cells in the brain work. These neurons grow so used to having the opiate around that they need it in order to function normally.

Researchers discovered how opiates create physical addiction by studying how they mimic the effects of endorphins in the brain. But the human brain and nervous system are very complicated and very delicate. Heroin and other opiates usually enter the body in amounts so great that the receptors are overloaded with false messages and are not able to handle the drug. One theory of addiction says that this overload is what forces the brain to change the way it works and become dependent on the drug.

But addiction doesn't end there. The body is tricked by high levels of heroin, and it stops producing endorphins. When the drug's effects wear off, the body does not resume producing endorphins, and the neurons become overactive. Eventually, these cells will work normally again, but in the meantime, they cause a wide range of painful symptoms in the brain and body. These are known as **withdrawal** symptoms.

If heroin is so dangerous, why do people use it? Some of the reasons are probably easy for you to understand. Kids may take drugs so that they can fit in with their peers (people their age) and be part of the "in" crowd. You may hear people explain that they use drugs because "everybody's doing it." Another reason is that the "high" heroin and other drugs cause may temporarily help to eliminate feelings of depression.

In some cases, people turn to drugs to escape feelings

or situations that they find intolerable. One important study of heroin addiction focused on U.S. soldiers who served in the Vietnam War during the 1960s and early 1970s. In Vietnam, heroin was easily available, and many soldiers used the drug to help them cope with the horrors of the war. In that atmosphere, many considered heroin use acceptable. When the soldiers returned to the United States, however, the situation was much different. They were no longer at war, but many had become addicted to heroin, which was much harder to get in the United States. In addition, the American public's attitude toward heroin users was very negative.

As a result, 90 percent of the soldiers who had used heroin in Vietnam completely stopped using it. They had no further psychological need for the drug. The other 10 percent, however, had become addicts. Even after they tried to stop, they had intense urges to use heroin and would often return to using the drug. They continued to use it despite the harm it was doing to their bodies, minds, and lives.

How does heroin addiction develop? Those who study the process have a number of theories about what causes it. In fact, addiction is probably caused by a wide range of physical and mental factors. In the next chapter, we'll look at what heroin does to the body and mind and why it can have such a powerful hold on those who use it.

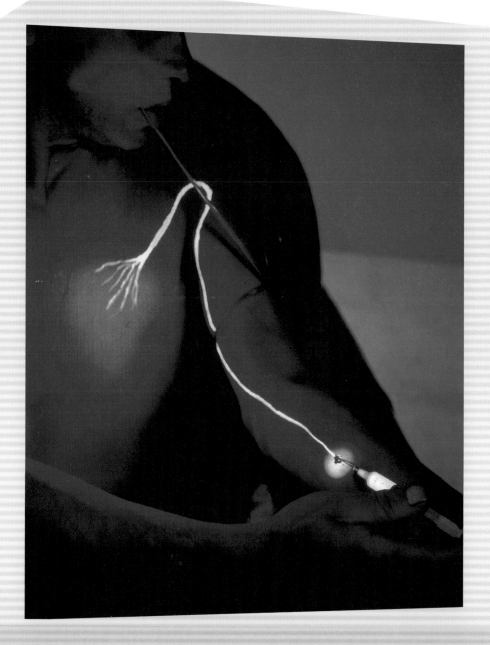

The yellow line in this illustration shows the direct path heroin takes to the heart after being injected. The user has tightened a band around the upper arm so that the vein swells and is easier to find with the needle. Injecting heroin is not the only way to become addicted to the drug, but it does carry additional dangers, such as damaged or infected veins, the risk of death from an air bubble, and the risk of becoming infected with HIV.

4 WHAT HEROIN DOES TO THE MIND AND BODY

We have already looked at the way heroin and other opiates such as opium, morphine, and codeine work in the body. Knowing the way a drug works is important information that can help you stay away from dangerous and harmful substances.

But people who are using or addicted to heroin don't think about neurons, endorphins, or opiate receptors. They are not thinking about the way chemicals and cells function but about the way heroin makes them *feel*.

How Do People Take Heroin?

Heroin can be taken in a number of ways. Until recently, the most popular way was by injecting dissolved heroin powder **intravenously,** or directly into the veins. This is the fastest way to get the drug into the bloodstream. Some users also try a method called "skin-popping." Instead of injecting heroin directly into a vein, they inject it **subcutaneously,** or into the tissue just under the surface of the skin.

In the past 10 years or so, snorting heroin—inhaling the powder through the nose—has become more popular among new users, in part because it is easier than injecting but also because some people mistakenly believe that they cannot become addicted to the drug unless they inject it. Others are worried about the risk of contracting **HIV,** the virus that causes **AIDS.** HIV can be transmitted through used hypodermic needles. (Read the article in this chapter about the danger of becoming infected with HIV when using heroin.) Heroin that has been snorted takes longer to produce a high because it has to travel through the mucous membranes in the nose to the blood vessels beneath.

What Does a Heroin User Feel?

All opiates—including those prescribed by physicians to relieve pain—cause a drowsy, pleasant state in which the user feels content and worry-free. Opiates relieve stress and discomfort by making a person feel detached, or cut off, from pain. A small, controlled dose of an opiate produces a range of mild effects than can aid a person who is suffering.

The effects produced by heroin are more immediately intense than those of any other opiate. Within seconds of injecting heroin, the user feels a powerful surge of pleasant, peaceful feelings throughout the body. This initial response is called a **rush** and lasts for a few min-

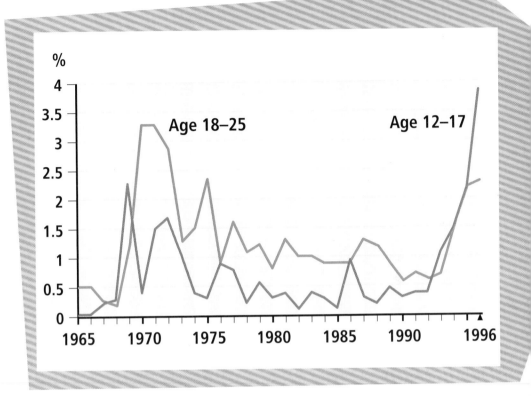

This graph, which covers the years 1965 to 1996, shows the number of people aged 12 to 17 and aged 18 to 25 who tried heroin for the first time. Look at the number of 12- to 17-year-olds who tried heroin in 1965 (lower left). The number is near zero. Now look at the number of kids in that age group who tried heroin in 1996. The number is almost 4 percent. A sharp rise occurred after 1990. Read Chapter 1 for some reasons why this happened.

utes. Although the user feels incredibly relaxed, this sensation can be very dangerous. If the dose of heroin is high enough, the body can "forget" to breathe and the brain can shut down, leading to coma or death.

Heroin's effects continue in a milder fashion for several hours after the initial rush. The user continues to

feel warm and relaxed, cut off from worries and desires. Feeling sleepy or lazy is common. Pulse and breathing rates slow down as well.

People who are high on heroin usually have poor coordination, slurred speech, and slow reactions. Their pupils are very small, their eyes may be watery, and their faces may be flushed. They may feel nauseated or vomit, especially if they are first-time users. This happens because the drug stimulates a part of the brain that causes vomiting when a toxic substance has been ingested.

Tolerance and Addiction

At first, even a small amount of heroin will have a powerful effect on a new user. However, as the person continues to abuse the drug, he or she will require greater amounts of the drug to cause the same powerful effect. In other words, the user has developed a tolerance to the drug. The brain senses an overload of opiates and stops producing endorphins. To continue functioning normally, the brain will require a greater supply of opiates.

When this happens, a heroin user has become physically dependent on the drug, or addicted. People who have been using heroin for a long time may develop a tolerance level so high that they can inject an amount that would kill a first-time user.

The danger of developing a tolerance to heroin is that eventually, the user will take such a large amount that he or she may overdose and die. If a heroin user stops taking the drug for a few months and then takes the same amount of the drug his or her body once had a tolerance to, an overdose may result.

Withdrawal

You may be surprised to learn how quickly a person can become addicted to heroin—it can take as little as two days. After that, according to the *Journal of the American Medical Association,* the user will experience painful withdrawal symptoms about 12 hours after the effects of the drug wear off. The body is no longer receiving the opiates it now requires to function normally. A heavy user will experience mild withdrawal symptoms almost as soon as the most recent dose wears off.

The symptoms of heroin withdrawal typically include muscle aches, sweating, chills, convulsions, and muscular spasms. Have you ever had the flu? If so, you have probably experienced similar symptoms. But withdrawal symptoms are much worse. A person can become **delirious** or experience **hallucinations** during withdrawal from heroin. It's a painful process that takes a long time. The symptoms usually peak within two days and ease in three to five days, although feelings of weakness may persist for weeks or months. But people addicted to heroin must go through this difficult and painful process if they want to escape the powerful hold the drug has over their lives.

Every heroin user experiences the same symptoms during withdrawal, but the length of time that a user has been taking the drug and the amount he or she is taking have an effect on how difficult the withdrawal process

A drug user prepares to inject heroin by melting the powder over
a flame and then pulling the liquid into a hypodermic needle.
To make more money from illegal sales, drug dealers sometimes
"cut" heroin with substances like sugar, flour, rat poison, or other
drugs, which increases the risk of infection or death.

becomes. For example, a heroin addict who has used the
drug several times a day for years will have greater difficulty kicking the habit than a user who took heroin a
few times in the previous month or two.

But withdrawal is extremely unpleasant in any case.
In fact, it can feel so awful that some people avoid it at
all costs. They continue to take heroin even though they
realize that the drug is destroying their lives and harm-

ing their bodies. To them, the pain of **detoxification** (ridding the body of toxic substances like drugs) is worse than all the negative aspects of taking heroin.

The Long-Term Dangers of Heroin Use

Using heroin over a long period of time can cause physical damage that is not directly related to the drug itself. For example, users who inject heroin often share hypodermic needles. If one of the users has a disease or infection such as HIV, tetanus, or hepatitis, the others using that dirty needle can become infected with the disease.

Another common problem among intravenous heroin users is damage to the veins. Injecting regularly can cause veins to collapse and infections to develop around the area of the collapsed vein. Addicts who are not careful or skilled in injecting can also kill themselves by accidentally injecting air into a vein. An air bubble in the bloodstream can reach the brain within a few seconds and cause death.

Another danger stems from the fact that heroin is an illegal drug and its quality and purity are therefore not controlled or regulated. A user's supply of heroin may be diluted, or "cut," so that the drug dealer can earn more money by stretching the supply. Sugar, caffeine, flour, and talcum powder are common substances added to heroin. Sometimes heroin is also cut with other drugs, which increases the possibility of an overdose. And if additives do not dissolve properly, they can clog blood vessels leading to the lungs, liver, kidneys, or brain and

(continued on p. 50)

Heroin Use and AIDS

It's a proven fact: if you use heroin intravenously (inject the drug into a vein), you run a high risk of being infected with the human immunodeficiency virus (HIV)—the virus that causes AIDS.

AIDS (acquired immunodeficiency syndrome) is caused when HIV has infected the body and diminished its natural immunity to disease. People who have AIDS are vulnerable to illnesses that rarely affect a person with a healthy immune system.

AIDS is often fatal. Before 1996, when new developments in drug treatment were discovered, contracting AIDS was considered a death sentence. Until that year, 85 to 90 percent of all AIDS patients died within three years. But the news in 1996 wasn't all good. That same year, a White House study reported that one in four new infections occurred among young people aged 13 to 20.

Intravenous drug users are the second-largest group at risk for contracting HIV. They make up about 25 to 30 percent of the total number of current AIDS cases. HIV cannot be passed by casual contact, such as shaking hands, hugging, or kissing on the cheek or on the lips; it can only be passed through infected blood, through sexual contact with an infected person, or from an infected mother to her baby. The disease is common among intravenous (or IV) drug users because addicts often share their hypodermic needles when "shooting up." Injecting leaves a tiny amount of blood on the needle—enough to transmit HIV to someone else who uses the same needle.

HIV can also be passed from an IV drug user to his or her sexual partners if the people involved practice unprotected sex (sex without a latex condom). Heroin and other drugs can also decrease users' inhibitions, leading them to do things they normally wouldn't do while "sober," such as engaging in unsafe sex. Because of the way HIV is transmitted, some people say that having unprotected sex with just one person is like engaging in sex with everyone that person has slept with.

The best way to protect yourself from HIV and AIDS is to avoid intravenous drug use and to abstain from sexual contact. If someone asks you to try heroin, just ask yourself: Is this worth dying for?

This chart shows the number of AIDS cases in the United States by "exposure category," meaning the way in which each person contracted HIV. Intravenous drug users make up the second-largest group of people who currently suffer from AIDS.

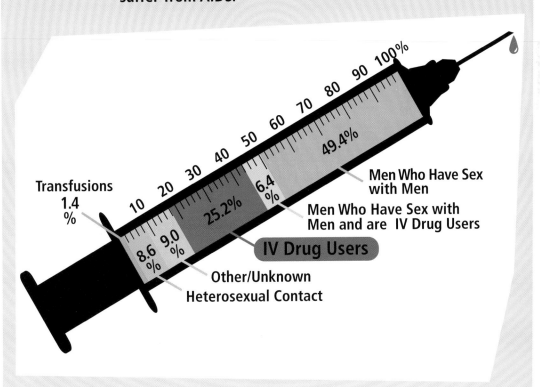

Transfusions 1.4 %

10 20 30 40 50 60 70 80 90 100%

49.4%

Men Who Have Sex with Men

6.4 %

Men Who Have Sex with Men and are IV Drug Users

25.2%

IV Drug Users

8.6 % 9.0 %

Other/Unknown

Heterosexual Contact

(continued from p. 47)

cause serious infections in those organs.

Heroin addicts are also especially at risk for developing mild to moderate depression. This disorder is usually characterized by insomnia (sleeplessness), an inability to concentrate, and feelings of extreme sadness, dejection, or hopelessness. Other psychological problems that can occur with long-term use of heroin include delirium, hallucinations or delusions, and mood swings. In most cases, these disorders can occur either during a high or during withdrawal.

In young women, heroin use may affect their ability to conceive children. The drug has been linked to serious complications like miscarriages and premature deliveries in women who do become pregnant. The children of women who were heroin addicts have a greater risk of dying from Sudden Infant Death Syndrome (SIDS), and they do not develop mentally and physically at the same pace as children of drug-free mothers.

If a woman becomes pregnant while addicted to heroin, trying to detoxify may increase her risk of miscarrying or having a premature delivery. For this reason, the expectant mother would most likely be treated with **methadone**—a drug similar to heroin that is commonly used to help addicts stop taking heroin.

Methadone treatment for the mother helps to ensure that the baby will be born safely. But did you know that babies of drug users can be born addicted to the drug? This is because during pregnancy, a growing fetus depends on its mother for nutrients, oxygen, and removal of wastes. The nutrients are passed through the mother's bloodstream to the fetus's bloodstream by way of the umbilical cord, which connects the mother to the child. If chemicals or drugs such as heroin are present in the mother's bloodstream, they can be passed to the fetus. When this happens, the newborn baby must also go through a withdrawal process before he or she can leave the hospital.

How can a person addicted to heroin become drug-free? It isn't easy, and it takes time, patience, and courage. We will read more about treatment methods for heroin addiction in Chapter 5.

Treating the mind: one of the most important elements of drug addiction treatment is psychological counseling. A former addict may see a counselor privately or meet with others in a group session, like the one shown here.

HOW TO TREAT HEROIN ADDICTION

t is very difficult for a heroin addict to kick his or her habit without getting help. As we read in Chapter 4, heroin not only causes intense withdrawal symptoms when a user tries to stop taking it, but it also creates a powerful psychological craving. A user not only feels bad without the drug; he or she also feels that there is only one "cure" for the awful symptoms—more heroin.

But there is hope for heroin users. A broad variety of programs in hospitals and clinics throughout North America are available to help them escape the drug's powerful hold. The programs do this not only by helping the user through the process of detoxification, or "detox," but also by providing support and therapy to help the user stay away from drugs for good.

Detoxification

Until the 1960s, detox alone was considered the best

way to treat heroin addiction. One method of detoxifying was to control and reduce the amount of heroin an addict used each day. Experts believed that the user's body would then gradually adapt to the absence of the drug and the withdrawal symptoms would be less severe. The alternative method was to stop heroin intake abruptly—a process known as quitting "cold turkey."

When detoxification was complete, former addicts were usually released from clinics without further treatment. But because this method was so difficult and did not address the strong cravings that remain after detoxification, many patients relapsed (returned to using heroin). Users often became caught up in a miserable cycle of addiction and detoxification that could last for years.

A Better Way to Treat Addiction

Today, detoxification is only the beginning step in the treatment of heroin addiction. In addition to administering milder drugs that help ease the pain of withdrawal, drug treatment centers provide counseling and psychotherapy to help the addict adjust to a drug-free life. To recover fully, the user must stop taking heroin as soon as the treatment program begins and must follow the detox process through to the very end.

The most common drug used to help heroin users end their addiction is methadone, a synthetic opioid that was developed during World War II as a substitute for morphine. Although methadone can also create dependence, it is not as addictive as morphine and heroin. In addition, the effects of methadone are longer-lasting but

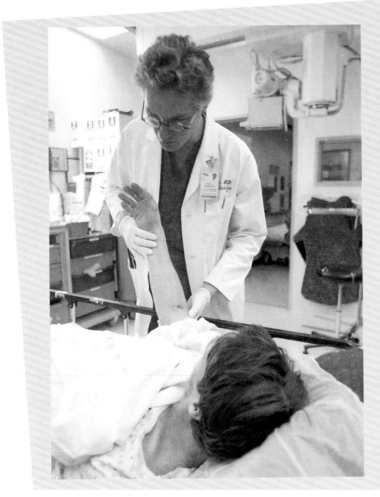

Treating the body: a San Francisco doctor examines a heroin addict who is being treated for abscesses (inflamed areas where pus has collected because of infection).

less intense than those of heroin. This is why it is viewed as an effective means of treating long-time addicts whose bodies require a constant supply of opiates.

If the proper dose is prescribed, methadone does not have the intoxicating effects of heroin and does not seem to interfere with everyday activities such as reading a newspaper or driving a car. However, because methadone is an opioid, it acts on the brain's opiate receptors in the same way that heroin or morphine does.

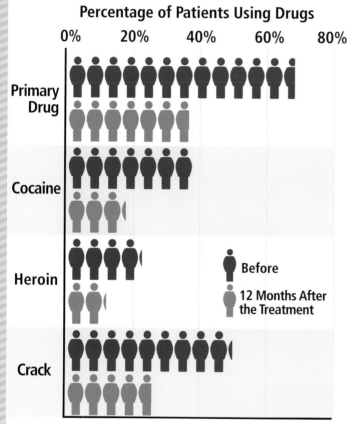

Percentage of Patients Using Drugs

Drug addiction treatment works. This chart shows the percentage of patients in a 1997 study who used drugs before getting treatment compared to the percentage who used drugs after getting treatment. The same study also showed decreases in criminal activity, high-risk behavior such as unsafe sex, and medical visits related to drug abuse.

Source: National Treatment Improvement Evaluation Study, Center for Substance Abuse Treatment, 1997

As a result, methadone "blocks" opiate receptor sites from receiving additional opiates. Even if a methadone patient tried to use heroin to experience a high, he or she would need an extremely strong dose to overcome the methadone block.

Methadone treatment allows the user to kick heroin without the usual intense withdrawal symptoms or cravings. Because methadone withdrawal creates much milder symptoms, and since methadone remains active in the body longer, the patient is able to function fairly normally between daily doses. With methadone treatment, heroin dependency can usually end in one to three weeks.

New Treatment Methods

In some heroin treatment centers, another drug that helps addicts kick their habit is becoming popular. The name of the drug is L-alpha-acetyl methadol, or **LAMM.** Like methadone, LAMM is a synthetic opioid that blocks heroin from linking to opiate receptors. But since the body metabolizes LAMM slowly, heroin users need to take it less frequently than methadone—three times a week, rather than every day. This is helpful for former addicts who are trying to lead drug-free lives. Dr. Paul Casadonte, the director of drug programs at the New York Veterans Affairs Medical Center, describes the difference between methadone and LAMM treatment: "LAMM patients don't feel hooked, so they want to get off of it," he says. "[Whereas] we have some people on [methadone] who have been using it 25 years."

One drawback of LAMM is that it doesn't take effect right away. It can also take several weeks before its effects stabilize (remain steady). And mixing LAMM with drugs or alcohol can be fatal, so addicts are at an even greater risk than normal if they should "slip" and return to drug using. But some people believe that it may one day replace methadone as the primary treatment for heroin addicts.

It is now possible to break heroin addiction even faster than with methadone or LAMM treatment. A very new and controversial program called "rapid detoxification" can complete detox within a day. How is this possible?

You may recall that in Chapter 3 we discussed a special group of drugs called opiate antagonists. The way these drugs work in the brain is similar to the way methadone works: they block opiate receptor sites. But opiate antagonists are different from methadone. They are not addictive, but they also do not have the painkilling or relaxing effects of opiates.

Opiate antagonists link more strongly to opiate receptors than opiates themselves can. (To understand how opiate antagonists work, imagine them pushing opiates out of their way to get to receptor sites first.) For years, doctors have used opiate antagonists in cases of heroin overdose because they work very quickly to revive the user. In rapid detoxification, doctors use opiate antagonists to rid a user's system of opiates within hours, rather than the days or weeks that standard detox requires. Because rapid detox works so quickly, an opiate antagonist is administered to the addict only while he or she is under anesthesia and avoids suffering from agonizing withdrawal symptoms.

Rapid detox is so new, however, that it has not been as thoroughly researched as other methods of drug addiction treatment. As a result, medical and scientific experts have varying opinions about rapid detoxification. Some believe that this method is better than methadone treatment because it does not involve the substitution of another drug and because it works so quickly.

Others are opposed to it because it has not been tested enough to be considered a safe treatment alternative. They also believe that the speed with which it works will give users the impression that it is an "easy" cure for heroin addiction. This might keep addicts from continuing to receive additional counseling after rapid detox is complete.

The Importance of Counseling for Heroin Addicts

Psychological counseling is a necessary final step in successful treatment of heroin addiction. For the most serious addict, a **therapeutic community** probably offers the best recovery strategy. In a therapeutic community, recovering addicts live for 6 to 24 months in a controlled setting where no drugs of any kind are permitted. The programs make use of the knowledge and insights of other addicts; in fact, they are often run by former addicts working with psychologists. While patients live in the treatment center, they may receive vocational and educational training to help them reenter the outside world more effectively. About 75 percent of residents leave therapeutic communities within the first six months, but 90 percent of those who stay for the full course of treatment are able to remain drug-free.

Another treatment method for heroin addiction is psychological counseling in a nonresidential (sometimes

called an **outpatient**) setting. The former addict meets with a therapist (often a psychiatrist) to discuss addiction and express his or her fears or misgivings. Sometimes former addicts will meet for group counseling, which allows them to tell their stories, discuss shared experiences, and support each other on the road to recovery.

Twelve-step programs, such as Narcotics Anonymous, work in much the same way. They are based on a program called Alcoholics Anonymous devised in 1935 by two men who were alcoholics and wanted to help others overcome their addiction. These groups are free and exist in almost every community (you can usually find them listed in your local phone book). Groups are usually made up entirely of recovering addicts who meet regularly to share advice and support each other. Each new member chooses a sponsor, who helps him or her follow certain steps to recovery and living a drug-free life. Twelve-step programs aim to help addicts gain a sense of control over their lives. They emphasize that individuals must learn to take their recovery "one day at a time." These programs also offer a safety net of understanding people they can turn to if they fear they will relapse.

No matter what treatment method is used, however, every addiction recovery program has the same goal: to help the addict become a healthy, functioning member of society and to encourage him or her to stay sober. Twelve-step programs, psychotherapy (meeting regularly with a psychologist or psychiatrist), and stays in therapeutic communities all fill this need.

As we have seen, heroin has a powerful hold over those who become addicted. But every heroin user can break these physical and psychological chains through treatment. To break an addiction and remain "clean" (drug-free), the user must also resolve to avoid people who still use drugs and develop a group of friends who support his or her efforts to remain clean. Just one slip can plunge a former heroin addict back into a cycle of dependence.

Everyone wants to be part of the crowd. But using drugs is not the way to fit in. Read this chapter for some ideas about how to stay away from drugs.

YOU CAN HELP

Now you know much more about the dangers of using heroin. Heroin can destroy or end your life. Users who don't die from the drug must go through a long and very painful process of withdrawal and therapy in order to return to a normal, drug-free life.

What does this tell you? The best thing is to avoid ever taking the drug in the first place.

Drugs and Peer Pressure

You have probably heard the term "peer pressure" before. Peers are classmates or friends about the same age who have similar backgrounds and interests. When these friends try to persuade you to do something, especially if it's something you know is wrong, such as shoplifting, vandalizing, or trying drugs, they are using peer pressure. It isn't always easy to spot, and kids don't always know that they're doing it. Everyone wants to fit

in, and friends who use peer pressure are just trying to be part of the crowd themselves.

For example, a schoolmate who wants you to try drugs might say "everyone does it" to convince you to do the same. Maybe kids who do drugs are considered the "in" crowd at your school, and others feel that they have to use drugs to fit in. Don't believe them. It's not "cool" to try drugs. It's just dumb. Using drugs or alcohol causes problems at school and at home. It makes you neglect things that are important to you—your family, your drug-free friends, your favorite activities.

It may *seem* as though everyone you know is using drugs, but that's not true. A national survey taken in 1997 showed that fewer than four percent of kids aged 12 and 13 are illegal drug users, and fewer than 20 percent of kids aged 16 and 17 take illegal drugs.

Turning down drugs is easier when you're not feeling pressure to try them. Here are a few ways to avoid being offered drugs:

Skip parties or activities where you know there will be alcohol or other drugs.

Hang out with friends who don't use drugs.

Find organized after-school activities. Check with recreation centers, youth clubs, libraries, or other local organizations to see whether they offer tutoring, sports, music lessons, or craft classes.

Get involved in drug-free activities, like dances, movies, or community service projects. Ask your friends to join you.

Organize a drug awareness program for your school, church, or community center.

Think about these figures in another way: that means that more than *96 percent* of 12- and 13-year-olds and more than *80 percent* of 16- and 17-year-olds are smart enough to stay away from drugs.

Once you look at it that way, you will realize that plenty of cool kids don't want to use or hang around with someone who uses drugs. Think about the long-term effects of using heroin—you'll have a high risk of contracting HIV, you'll have lots of physical problems, and you'll feel lousy most of the time. And even if you decide to stop, you'll have a tough road ahead before you're drug-free.

Then ask yourself: would a *real* friend offer you something that could do all of that to you?

How Can I Tell if Someone I Know Is Using Drugs?

Even if you've never tried heroin or other drugs and never intend to, you may know someone who has. How can you tell whether someone has a problem with drugs? Here are a few signs to look for:

- Getting high or drunk on a regular basis
- Lying about the amount of alcohol or other drugs used
- Avoiding you or other friends to get high or drunk
- Giving up activities, such as sports, homework, or hanging out with friends who don't drink or use other drugs
- Having to increase the amount of drugs used to get the same effect

Learning the signs of heroin or other drug use is one way you can help someone who has a drug problem.

- Constantly talking about drinking or using other drugs
- Pressuring other people to drink alcohol or use other drugs
- Believing that he or she needs to drink or use other drugs to have fun
- Getting into trouble with the law or getting suspended from school for an alcohol- or other drug-related incident
- Taking risks, including sexual risks and driving under the influence of alcohol or other drugs
- Feeling tired, run-down, hopeless, depressed, or even suicidal

- Missing work or school, or performing tasks poorly

Keep in mind that some of these signs, such as mood changes, difficulty getting along with others, poor job or school performance, and depression, might be signs of other problems, such as an illness that you may not know about.

How Can I Tell if Someone I Know Is Using Heroin?

There are specific signs that someone is under the influence of heroin or another opiate. Here are the most common ones:

- Abnormally constricted pupils
- Frequent scratching
- Extreme sleepiness or repeated drowsing off
- Puncture marks in the skin, especially the arms
- The presence of drug **paraphernalia** (hypodermic needles or other equipment used to prepare or inject heroin)

If you think that a friend is on drugs, you should tell an adult whom you trust—a parent or other relative, teacher, school counselor, coach, or religious leader. This may be difficult, but it is the best way to help your friend. If your friend does get help and is trying to stop using drugs, be sure to continue supporting him or her during, and especially after, treatment is completed. No one should or can face the challenge of recovery alone.

addiction—a condition of some drug users that is caused by repeated drug use. An addicted user continues to take drugs, despite severe negative consequences. Obtaining and using the drug take over the person's life.

AIDS—acquired immune deficiency syndrome; a defect of the immune system caused by the human immunodeficiency virus (HIV). AIDS is spread by the exchange of blood and by sexual contact; intravenous drug users have an increased risk of contracting HIV and developing AIDS.

alkaloid—any of the various basic and bitter compounds containing nitrogen that are found in seed plants. Morphine and codeine are alkaloids.

brain stem—the part of the brain that connects the spinal cord with the cerebrum, thalamus, and hypothalamus. The brain stem controls what your body does automatically, such as coughing and breathing.

codeine—a pain-relieving agent found in opium that is related to morphine but is less potent. Codeine is used in some prescription cough remedies.

delirium—a mental disturbance characterized by confusion, disordered speech, and hallucinations. Delirium is one of the symptoms of opiate withdrawal.

detoxification—the process by which an opiate-addicted person is gradually withdrawn from the drug. This is usually done under medical supervision, and sometimes includes other drugs such as methadone.

diacetylmorphine—the chemical name of heroin.

endorphin—a substance produced in the brain that attaches to receptor sites on neurons. Endorphins help regulate the body's responses to stress, pain, and other internal and external events that affect one's well-being. Opiates like heroin and morphine mimic the pain-relieving and euphoric effects of endorphins.

hallucination—an object or vision that is not real, but is perceived by a person who has a mental disorder or who is using drugs.

heroin—the trade name given to diacetylmorphine, one of the strongest of the opiate drugs. Some street names for heroin are "H," "horse," "smack," "junk," and "black tar."

HIV—human immunodeficiency virus; the virus that causes AIDS.

intravenous—introduced into the body through a vein.

LAMM—L-alpha-acetyl methadol; a long-acting form of methadone that is used to treat some heroin addicts.

laudanum—an opium preparation that was once considered a cure-all for a number of painful ailments and was sold in pharmacies as medicine.

limbic system—the part of the brain that controls emotion and motivation.

methadone—an opioid developed in Germany during World War II as a less addictive substitute for morphine. Methadone produces less intense but longer-lasting effects than heroin or morphine and is commonly used to treat addiction to the two drugs.

morphine—an opiate developed at the beginning of the 19th century. Morphine was first used as a pain reliever and later as a recreational drug before its addictive properties were understood.

neuron—a nerve cell.

neurotransmitter—a chemical, such as an endorphin, that is released by neurons and carries messages between them.

opiate—a drug derived from the milky juice of the poppy plant. Opiates include opium, morphine, codeine, and heroin.

opiate antagonist—a substance that links with opiate receptors in the brain and blocks the effects of opiates such as heroin and morphine. Unlike opioids such as methadone, opiate antagonists are not addictive or mood-altering.

opiate receptor—a kind of receptor site that links to opiates or opioids. Opiate receptors are concentrated in certain parts of the brain, including the limbic system and brain stem.

opioid—a synthetic drug devised to produce effects similar to opiates. Methadone is an opioid.

outpatient—a patient who visits a hospital, clinic, or other facility for treatment but is not required to check in.

Papaver somniferum—Latin for "sleep-inducing poppy"; the scientific name for the poppy plant from which opiates are distilled.

paraphernalia—devices or equipment, such as hypodermic needles, strainers, spoons, and rubber tubing, that are used to prepare or inject illegal drugs.

physical dependence—also as known as addiction, a state in which a drug user's body chemistry has adapted to require regular doses of the drug to function normally. Stopping the drug causes withdrawal symptoms. Opioids cause severe physical dependence.

psychological dependence—the state of addiction in which certain brain changes create strong cravings to use a drug, even if the user has no withdrawal symptoms or physical urge to do so. Opioids cause severe psychological dependence.

predisposed—having a tendency toward a particular action or thing. Some people are predisposed to develop drug addictions.

receptor site—a special area of a cell that combines with a chemical substance to alter the cell's function.

rush—a powerful surge of pleasurable feelings that occurs immediately after injecting heroin.

speedball—a mixture of heroin and cocaine that is injected into the body through a vein.

subcutaneous—under the surface of the skin.

synapse—a gap between neurons through which neurotransmitters carry messages.

therapeutic community—a treatment center for recovering drug addicts that is drug-free and often run by former addicts working with psychologists.

tolerance—the body's ability to endure or become less responsive to a drug. A user needs increasingly large amounts of the drug to achieve the same level of "high."

twelve-step program—a drug users' support program in which former addicts gather regularly to share advice. Each twelve-step program member chooses a "sponsor," who helps the member take specific steps toward recovery. Examples of twelve-step programs are Alcoholics Anonymous (AA) and Narcotics Anonymous (NA).

withdrawal—a process that occurs when a person who is physically dependent on a drug stops taking the drug. Withdrawal from heroin and other opiates causes physical symptoms similar to a bad case of the flu, including muscle aches and cramps, fever, vomiting, and weakness. It also causes mental symptoms such as depression and hallucinations.

BIBLIOGRAPHY

Cox, Christopher. *Chasing the Dragon: Into the Heartland of the Golden Triangle.* New York: Henry Holt, 1997.

Hutchings, Donald. *Methadone: Treatment for Addiction.* New York: Chelsea House Publishers, 1992.

Lockley, Paul. *Counseling Heroin and Other Drug Users.* New York: New York University Press, 1995.

National Clearinghouse for Alcohol and Drug Information (NCADI), Center for Substance Abuse Prevention. *Drugs of Abuse.* NCADI Publication No. RP0926. Rockville, MD: NCADI, 1998.

———. *Straight Facts About Drugs and Alcohol.* Rockville, MD: NCADI, 1998.

National Institute on Drug Abuse (NIDA). *Heroin Abuse and Addiction.* NIH Publication NO. 97-4165. Bethesda, MD: NIDA, 1997.

———. *Mind Over Matter: The Brain's Response to Opiates.* NIH Publication No. 97-3856. Bethesda, MD: NIDA, 1997.

Simpson, Carolyn. *Methadone.* New York: Rosen Publishing, 1997.

Substance Abuse and Mental Health Services Administration (SAMHSA). *The Changing Face of Heroin: Teenagers at Risk.* Publication No. SMA 97-3126. Rockville, MD: Department of Health and Human Services, 1997.

Zackon, Fred. *Heroin: The Street Narcotic.* New York: Chelsea House Publishers, 1992.

FIND OUT MORE ABOUT HEROIN, DRUG ADDICTION, AND AIDS

The following list includes agencies, organizations, and websites that provide information about heroin, other drugs, and AIDS. You can also find out where to go for help with a drug problem.

Many national organizations have local chapters listed in your phone directory. Look under "Drug Abuse and Addiction" to find resources in your area.

Agencies and Organizations in the United States

American Council for Drug Education
164 West 74th Street
New York, NY 10023
212-758-8060
800-488-DRUG
http://www.acde.org/
wlittlefield@phoenixhouse.org

Center for Substance Abuse Treatment
Information and Treatment Referral Hotline
11426-28 Rockville Pike, Suite 410
Rockville, MD 20852
800-662-HELP (4357)

Hazelden Foundation/Pleasant Valley Road
P.O. Box 176
Center City, MN 55012
800-328-9000

Heroin Help Line
800-9HEROIN (437646)

Narcotics Anonymous
P.O. Box 9999
Van Nuys, CA 91409
818-780-3951

National Center on Addiction and Substance Abuse at Columbia University
152 West 57th Street, 12th Floor
New York, NY 10019-3310
212-841-5200
212-956-8020
http://www.casacolumbia.org/home.htm

National Clearinghouse for Alcohol and Drug Information (NCADI)
P.O. Box 2345
Rockville, MD 20847-2345
301-468-2600
800-729-6686
http://www.health.org/pubs.htm

National Council on Alcoholism and Drug Dependence
12 West 21st Street, 7th Floor
New York, NY 10010
800-622-2255

National Families in Action
2296 Henderson Mill Road, Suite 300
Atlanta, GA 30345
404-934-6364

Office of National Drug Control Policy
750 17th Street, N.W., Eighth Floor
Washington, DC 20503
http://www.whitehousedrugpolicy.gov/
ondcp@ncjrs.org
888-395-NDCP (6327)

Parents Resource Institute for Drug Education (PRIDE)
3610 Dekalb Technology Parkway, Ste 105
Atlanta, GA 30340
770-458-9900
Fax: 770-458-5030
http://www.prideusa.org/

Agencies and Organizations in Canada

Addictions Foundation of Manitoba
1031 Portage Avenue
Winnipeg, Manitoba R3G 0R8
204-944-6277
Fax: 204-728-0225
http://www.mbnet.mb.ca/crm/health/
afm.html

Addiction Research Foundation (ARF)
33 Russell Street
Toronto, Ontario M5S 2S1
416-595-6100
800-463-6273 in Ontario

Alberta Alcohol and Drug Abuse Commission
10909 Jasper Avenue, 6th Floor
Edmonton, Alberta T5J 3M9
http://www.gov.ab.ca/aadac/

British Columbia Prevention Resource Centre
96 East Broadway, Suite 211
Vancouver, British Columbia V5T 1V6
604-874-8452
Fax: 604-874-9348
800-663-1880 (British Columbia only)

Canadian Centre on Substance Abuse
75 Albert Street, Suite 300
Ottawa, Ontario K1P 5E7
613-235-4048
Fax: 613-235-8101
http://www.ccsa.ca/

Ontario Healthy Communities Central Office
180 Dundas Street West, Suite 1900
Toronto, Ontario M5G 1Z8
416-408-4841
Fax: 416-408-4843
http://www.opc.on.ca/ohcc/

Saskatchewan Health Resource Centre

Saskatchewan Health, T.C. Douglas Building
3475 Albert Street
Regina, Saskatchewan S4S 6X6
306-787-3090
Fax: 306-787-3823

AIDS Hotlines

National AIDS Hotline
English: 800-342-AIDS
Spanish: 800-344-SIDA
TDD Service: 800-243-7889

National AIDS Clearinghouse
800-458-5231

American Foundation for AIDS Research (AMFAR)
800-392-6327

AIDS Treatment Data Network
212-268-4196

Websites

Center for Alcohol & Addiction Studies (CAAS)
http://www.caas.brown.edu/

D.A.R.E. (Drug Abuse Resistance Education) for Kids
http://www.dare-america.com/index2.htm

Drug Strategy Institute
http://www2.druginfo.org/orgs/dsi/

National Institute on Drug Abuse (NIDA)
http://www.nida.nih.gov/

Partnership for a Drug-Free America
http://www.drugfreeamerica.org/

PBS Frontline documentary: The Opium Kings
http://www.pbs.org/wgbh/pages/frontline/shows/heroin/

Despite what you may have heard,
selling illegal drugs will not make you rich.

In 1998, two professors, Steven Levitt from the University of Chicago and Sudhir Venkatesh from Harvard University, released a study of how drug gangs make and distribute money. To get accurate information, Venkatesh actually lived with a drug gang in a midwestern city.

You may be surprised to find out that the average street dealer makes just about $3 an hour. You'd make more money working at McDonald's! Still think drug-dealing is a cool way to make money? What other after-school jobs carry the risk of going to prison or dying in the street from a gunshot wound?

Drug-dealing is illegal, and it kills people. If you're thinking of selling drugs or you know someone who is, ask yourself this question: is $3 an hour worth dying for or being imprisoned?

WHAT A DRUG GANG MAKES IN A MONTH*

	During a Gang War	No Gang War
INCOME (money coming in)	$ 44,500	$ 58,900
Other income (including dues and blackmail money)	10,000	18,000
TOTAL INCOME	**$ 54,500**	**$ 76,900**
EXPENSES (money paid out)		
Cost of drugs sold	$ 11,300	$ 12,800
Wages for officers and street pushers	25,600	37,600
Weapons	3,000	1,600
Tributes (fees) paid to central gang	5,800	5,900
Funeral expenses	2,300	800
Other expenses	8,000	3,400
TOTAL EXPENSES	**$ 56,000**	**$ 62,100**
TOTAL INCOME	$ 54,500	$ 76,900
MINUS TOTAL EXPENSES	- 56,000	- 62,100
TOTAL AMOUNT OF PROFIT IN ONE MONTH	**- 1,500**	**14,800**

* adapted from "Greedy Bosses," *Forbes*, August 24, 1998, p. 53.
Source: Levitt and Venkatesh.

INDEX

PICTURE CREDITS

JIM GALLAGHER is the author of several books for young adults. A former newspaper editor and publisher, he lives near Philadelphia.

BARRY R. McCAFFREY is Director of the Office of National Drug Control Policy (ONDCP) at the White House and a member of President Bill Clinton's cabinet. Before taking this job, General McCaffrey was an officer in the U.S. Army. He led the famous "left hook" maneuver of Operation Desert Storm that helped the United States win the Persian Gulf War.

STEVEN L. JAFFE, M.D., received his psychiatry training at Harvard University and the Massachusetts Mental Health Center and his child psychiatry training at Emory University. He has been editor of the *Newsletter of the American Academy of Child and Adolescent Psychiatry* and chairman of the Continuing Education Committee of the Georgia Psychiatric Physicians' Association. Dr. Jaffe is professor of child and adolescent psychiatry at Emory University. He is also clinical professor of psychiatry at Morehouse School of Medicine, and the director of Adolescent Substance Abuse Programs at Charter Peachford Hospital in Atlanta, Georgia.